BUT I PREVAIL

BUT I PREVAIL

Alaa Taha

BUT I PREVAIL

This book is a work of fiction.

Copyright © 2022 by Alaa Taha

www.alaataha.com

*For my past self: for all the love she gave
and the hurt she endured.*

*And to Fatima, Chloe, and Seuraya: thank you for
your encouragement and support.*

part one
the love

Ever Afters

Garden gnomes and pathways
to a euphoric ever after.
Picnic lunch and sun rays
with juvenile teasing and laughter.
Lounging at water springs
yellow flowers and engagement rings
and 'til death do us part.

We share a new home now,
just us two. We light crimson candles,
set the mood. My highbrow
lover, and quiet talks of scandals.
Cuddles and butterflies
while we play violin melodies,
I count hues in your eyes.
Faultless smile, you watch me, breathlessly.

There is nowhere else I would rather be.
Let us linger here, in love and carefree.

Love At First Sight

It was not love at first sight.
She was too stubborn, despite
her romantic delusions.
Their lighthearted conclusions
of their favorite childhood
chapter books, old neighborhoods.
A surge of bare optimism,
a sharp form of escapism,
twist through her anatomy.

She slowly falls in love while
lying on a field–an aisle
of purple hibiscus. Chaste
kisses, thoughts. Hands on her waist.
A voice whispers in her ear,
"Stay with me forever." Here,
she flutters her eyes shut, pleased.
Brown eyes glimmer in her mind.

Sweet Pepperidge Tree

The sun's glow scorches,
and our eyes crinkle
from heat and delight.
Your soft eyes twinkle
with warmth and daylight.

Our frequent garden trips
that last forevermore.
An innocuous grip
like a fawn in the spring.
Tulips sprout in the grass,
you push me on the swing.

Our secrets, like the bridge
just over the river,
past the sweet pepperidge
tree, confectionary candy.

My dear, I'm paper,
you're glue.
There is no other
but you.

All Mine

Your cocoa brown eyes and scenic lakes,
idyllic smiles and buoyancy for our sakes.
Abrupt, damning lies and secret spies
to precipitate our heartrending demise.
Keen desires of future proposals
and much disapprovals at our disposal.

It is unimaginably vile,
living an egocentric lifestyle.
My creative essence, lifelong dreams
dissipates before my grisly screams.
A little caterpillar hoping
to evolve, is vetoed. My coping
apparatus finds itself in you.
Is it wrong? Perhaps, but take me too.

A cabin where we can be marooned
is all I really need. Attuned
to your demeanor, and scant facets
that you quite hate, but I don't. Glasses
perched on your nose, to read poetic
verses and prose beneath aesthetic
fairy lights and fireflies. You're all mine.

Saltwater
Surprises

Your baby blue eyes
were my sweetest surprise.
Recall ocean waves,
hued underwater caves.
You matched my rich tone,
with odes and high cheekbones.

Footsteps on the sand,
your back—hot and tanned.
Your dark locks of hair,
shamelessly, I stare.
Pebbles and seashells,
and glee and pastels.

Saltwater rolls down
your broad chest. I drown
in the sacred sight
of sinful delight.

To Never Be Taken from Me

Raven locks cascade across your snowy cheeks
as you watch the sunset past the frosty peaks.
A sight to behold: your gentle respiration,
eyebrows wrinkled and lips pressed in contemplation.
A visual to never be taken from me.

Eyes trailing across stripped bodies, and closed doors.
A hand softly caresses my neck; It's yours.
Dominos toppling for a lifetime and a half,
the anguish I endured; a sanguine epigraph.
A fantasy to never be taken from me.

A wiry frame accompanies clever quips,
a philosophical age of scholarships.
Chocolate orbs scrutinize my entire being.
Lips part, I wonder, "Does he like what he's seeing?"
An impression to never be taken from me.

WHAT DO WE
HAVE TO LOSE

French patio doors and balcony rendezvous
Intermingled arms and sunrises of orange hues.
Taken day by day in a field of red tulips.
Your nose nudges my neck, hands pressed into my hips.

Marvelous outings to Carnegie Hall and art galleries
and my heart soars whenever you ask for me.
It takes two to know one, and one to form a bold fixation.
We fill our nights with stars and constellations.

We hoped they would accept us—me and you,
for what we felt for one another was purely true
But times are tough, people are hard to please.
So we don't, for their twisted verdicts are a disease.

Thus, I erased them from my mind, abolished their crude views.
All is left is you and I, what else have we got to lose?
From fire, muses and devotion seem to only arise.
I'd trade them for you, an inevitable compromise.

part two
the hurt

i
confess

Riveting hurricanes
and suffocating chains
That leave me to wonder,
in the thick of thunder
and this disastrous flood,
"Was it worth all the blood
and pain you had caused me?"

Thick as a garden's vines,
delicate as landmines.
Me, thinking of the mess
we made. And I confess,
truly, I trusted this.
Tears shed, I reminisce.
Forlorn, I guarantee.

A Lament of Bloodshed

No other man could charm me like him, but he's gone.
My locket, his photo, remind me he's moved on
to a new woman: lighter hair, a slimmer frame.
Maybe he got tired of me, of this grande dame.
I would have severed my arm to bestow him joy.
Would have gladly surrendered and watched him destroy
Me. In turn, he would have kicked me while I was down.
No more scarlet flowers, or stripping dressing gowns.

There is a single rose waiting to prick my skin.
I grip it tightly, blood trickles out from within.
There is only so much hurt a woman can take
before her heart breaks in four, and her muscles ache.
There is a riddle that leaves me in disarray,
the rotting of my garden since he went away.
Time may never mend me, nor shall it ever try,
A foolish girl with a romantic lullaby.

You give your heart to someone,
then they change their mind.

It is pain you can't outrun,
quite self-disinclined.
Umpteen chances are given,
and chances are tossed.
First, mistakes are forgiven
then some lines get crossed.

Ocean waves get overturned.
You live and you bleed,
and then you bleed and you burn.
Like waves, we proceed
back and forth, from fire to ash.
Then gone with a flash.

Without mere alterations,
we struggle and strive.
Our simple expectations
would never survive.
White candle wicks, and wax drips
onto hardwood floors.
Stains on our relationships,
like fabled world wars.

You Give Your Heart to Someone...

Reconsider life changes,
a piano song.
Re-examine exchanges
and where you belong.
When it is time, I ensure
you'll thrive and mature.

You give your heart to someone,
then you change your mind.

Flashback
Reflections

You pulled out my chair
the first time we met.
Our secret affair,
or did you forget?

Your smile, sweet and quite warm.
I hid behind my fringe.
Your perfect little storm.
I burned blush and cheeks singed.

And I still think about you
even when you have moved on.
I hope you think of me too,
in daylight, when you are gone.

Months of your false smile
twenty million times.
My heart turned as vile
as your dirty crimes.

I thought we would last for life.
And I held on to the hope
that you would combat the strife
even through our lowest slope.

Her shoulder was wrapped under your arm
laughing out loud at your absurd jokes
and in awe at your peculiar charm,
and your bad habit of midnight smokes.

TAKE ME BACK

My lonely soul sought
out a distraction.
A fair reaction
that momma worried
For me. I hurried
to veil this affair,
for it was all I could do.

The way his lingering stares
tested my patience,
brought an oasis
to my lonely plain.

This thrilling expansion
shooting straight to my heart.
A reggae atlantan
bar, we sit inches apart.

The crumpling of paper
like the squeezing of my bones.
And a crumbling skyscraper,
like my chest weighted with stones.

temporary playthings

Do you still think about me, too?
What is it you miss, if you do?
Do you grieve me the way I do you?
If I asked, would you lie to me, too?

Poetic verses and heartfelt prose.
Lilac dandelions, a gold rose.
Indubitably rare, like this fling.
Red lips and temporary playthings.
Silent echoes chase my thoughts away.
Dreamless, sleepless nights, and haunted days.

If I said we had it good, would you agree?
Would you turn around and run straight back to me?
Or would you rush away like I wasn't worth it?
Or swallow your pride and confess, please admit.

Starry eyes and rose-colored glasses,
razor-edged knives and fatal fasces.
Flowers wither like my spoiled soul,
purely ebony and charcoal.

An Intrusion

Grief pulls me apart.
The flesh of my limbs
a blade in my heart,
my mind, bleak and grim.
A crack in my bones.
The tear in my soul
is like a cyclone
that rips a whole
city, desecrating what once was.

OBSCURE RELATIONS

Solitary subsisting,
and a harsh reminder that
I'm better off on my own.
Lonely lays my sole tombstone.

Disgraced conviction, they say,
"You love too much." And I do.
Cross my heart, lost it halfway
at only twenty-two.

A little fool, I am, perhaps,
falling into that. The healing
cycle ensues, then my relapse.
Pain grinds my bones, a concealing
powder of blue, controls my every move.

Breakfast toast and unplanned coffee breaks.
A synchronic match made in heaven
and celestial lunches by the lakes.
Lights her cigarettes, nearly seven.
Opposing pasts and merging futures.

Time wasted, a distant recollection
left me powerless to my very core.
By my lonesome, a paltry reflection
of a barren desert lacking downpour.
Midnight pacing, judging, mind erasing.

Why do we befriend others when we are doomed to fall?
We strive to carry ourselves out of the cold rubble,
then trust one another, a repeated protocol.
My mother warned me on the first day. "She is trouble,"
she had said. I refused to listen and lost my head.

I fail to understand this foreign spectacle.
She was truly my only sister, my comrade.
No love was greater. An empty receptacle,
I became. She renounced me like a deadbeat dad.
Now I must arise from my grave to start anew.

RECORDS Play On

Your breath heats my lips
as you whisper sweet words.
A lunar eclipse
sets the tone. Our records
play on.

My guilty pleasures
come in the form of
thinking about what
could've been.
Protective measures
to guard me from love.
Reminisce about
past events
that made my head spin.

The potent aroma of my perfume
takes me back to wildflowers and dark eyes.
When unconditional desire consumed
me. Pining gazes at you, clear gray skies.

Round drops of condensation
roll down the sides of your glass.
A wet ring stains the foundation
of this table, like you stained the brass
foundation of this little affair.

broken

Sadistic black eyes pin me to the spot
illuminated by a candle's bright flame.
A vitriolic kind of juggernaut
that devastates everything in its frame,
expecting you to exculpate the blows.

Your words cut me
and broke the skin.
I feared the cage
you put me in.

Those dark rooms and
my broken bones.
Silent screams, grand
wistful headstones.

To off myself from the
coldness of your black soul
would be far too simple.
To resign that control
would be self-destructive.

My undermined heart liquified into
a ring of lava. A gaping hollow
hole in its place. The walls—ebony blue,
caging me in, a reticent wallow
In fear of judgments and I-told-you-so's

.

Vanished Sentiments

A trail of love letters straight to your door,
a clutter of warm sweaters by the score.
A shot of your face seared into my mind,
a form of recollections to unwind.

With glasses gently perched upon your nose.
With fixated spotlights and dazzling glows.
With dandelion seeds and telling cues,
with summer sun and then December blues.

And no more wills to try and no more ways,
and no more plans to make; illicit phase.
No more woes or withheld secrets to tell,
no more us, you, or feelings to expel.

part three
the revival

BUT I PREVAIL

Webs of white crawl across my skin
and the arches I tend to veil
with coats and hunched dispositions.
Condemn the gentle and forceful
leaders to a simplified role.
But I resist.

Nicks of red emerge on milky
limbs to attain feigned perfection.
Time unwinds as my past haunts me.
Mistakes seek to impair my grit,
among ghosts who hide in the night.
But I resist.

Weight fluctuates and skin creases
with age. Criticize the dear souls
that shelter mankind's destiny.
Their words extinguish my self-worth
to make them augment their self-worth.
But I prevail.

Delicate Glass

I have grown weary of wilting, viewed as not enough.
The world out there is callous, almost far too rough.
Vigorous bursts of wind jostle my trees from their roots,
burnished windows shatter from repeated pursuits.
These shards of delicate glass scattered across the floor
I trusted myself, did not budge, forevermore.

I trudge from pillar to post with a shell shielding me.
Dead leaves, twisted branches, living insipidly.
I hide when I am afraid, to keep myself secure.
Truly, was I amiss? Was I wrong to ensure
my precious safety? But did I grow when I couldn't breathe?
Did I blossom when I was diligently sheathed?

I must escape this shell of protection
and elude a life of sheer deception.
It is solely my prized obligation
to procure a life of exultation.

We Are Only Men

A speck in a land, great and wide
fighting our battles side by side.
But when the stars shift, and the waves collide,
we triumph in weakness by a landslide.

A kind of frailty flows through our bloodlines,
and with frailty arises brittle spines.
Stability and strength, we all seem to lack,
the world of you and I is not white nor black.

And when our days become frequently trying,
our own demons emerge, with liars lying.

A sole grain could swiftly destroy the eye.
Calling ourselves heroes: to do or die.
These men are not kings but clowns underneath.
This eludes my mind, I gravely bequeath.

Darling, mankind repeats the same mistakes.
Their ancestries' faults are their own keepsakes.
Then we fail to learn from living our lives,
despite historical files and archives.

It's blurred and uncharted territory,
don't you see? This tale, a desultory
approach to growing civilizations.
Humanity has renounced its stations.

To proceed down this path will lead to annihilation,
with the wrath of strangers from countries of fabrication.

And so, how does hate develop within a heart?
Is it the pain of existing that tears it apart?
Is it the wearying cycle of endless abuse?
The first is mistreated, the second is misused.

Now I wonder: is it too complex to pass along a rose?
To a neighbor, a friend, and perhaps your foes?
Or will we forever follow leaders who lead us astray?
Toward hate, cruelty, and into the gray.

Time will determine, but even then, I presume
most of humankind will end up consumed
by ludicrous delusions: they are all supreme.
A mystical, superpower regime.

My Mother Holds Me

My mother holds me in her arms,
gripping tightly with reason.
She promises: whoever harms
her pearl, born in the season
of Summer, will endure her rage.

I am ten now.

I watch my schoolmates disappear down the steep pathway
from the backseat of my mother's car. I meet her eyes.
"Why can't I go with them?" I ask her on a Friday.
My mother warns me of threats with logic that defies.
I am not trusted enough.

She drops me off at school
with a kiss and my lunch.
I envy those girls, so cruel
to me. A blonde haired, brown eyed bunch.
I am not good enough.

My friends knock on my door and tell me to come out.
I ask mother, "Can I go now? Can I play?"
She tells me to be careful when running about,
and to be mindful of watching eyes that prey
on girls like me.
I don't understand enough.

I am twenty now.

My mother tells me not to stay out too late.
Disgruntled, I tell her I can't be confined.
My longing for freedom and to stay past eight
torments me even after I have resigned.
My mother doesn't understand enough.

I am a mother now.

I hold my daughter in my arms,
gripping tightly with reason.
I understand enough.

tbc…